The City of Amsterdam, Netherlands, Holland

Twenty-five beautiful Color Views

from 1890-1900

with descriptions

The City of Amsterdam, Netherlands, Holland
Twenty-five beautiful Color Views from 1890-1900 with descriptions

Copyright © 2016 D. M. Kalten

You do have permission to duplicate a
view for your personal family history work.
A reference is appreciated.

Forward

The views shown in this book are from 1890 to 1900.

They are placed to give you the largest view possible.

...

This book actually came into existence due to a family history project. If you had family in Amsterdam in the late 1800s to early 1900s, this is what was familiar to them.

...

As the views are in color, it greatly affects the publishing cost and unfortunately no author can control that. It was decided to publish as these views are wonderful for use with family history projects.

...

Dam Square with the Nieuwe Kerk (new church) on the left.
ca 1890 -1900 Amsterdam

Blue Bridge and Amstel River ca 1890-1900 Amsterdam

De Oude Schans ca 1890-1900 Amsterdam

Fishmarket and bourse (i.e. Weighing house) on right.

Originally a gate in the city walls. Now a subway station, Nieuwmarkt. 1890-1900 Amsterdam

Groen Burgwal (canal) ca 1890-1900 Amsterdam

Kloveniersburgwal (canal) ca 1890-1900 Amsterdam

Mint Tower ca 1890-1900 Amsterdam

Museum 1890 Amsterdam

Nicolaaskerk (St. Nicholas Church) 1890 Amsterdam

Prince Henry's Quay ca 1890-1900 Amsterdam

The Binnen Amstel (inner Amstel) ca 1890-1900 Amsterdam

The Buiten Amstel ca 1890-1900 Amsterdam

The Great Sluice ca 1890-1900 Amsterdam

The Heerengracht (main canal) ca 1890-1900 Amsterdam

A Kolk (canal) ca 1890-1900 Amsterdam

The New Market and Bourse ca 1890-1900.
Originally this was the Kloveniersburgwal canal and De Waag (weighing house). Originally a gate in the city walls and now is a subway station, Nieuwmakt. Amsterdam.

The Post Office ca 1890-1900 Amsterdam

The Square, Palace and Church ca 1890-1900 Amsterdam

The Station – 1890 Amsterdam

Oudezijds Voorburgwal & Sint Nicolaaskerk (Church of St. Nicholas) ca 1890-1900 Amsterdam